BELIEFS AND CULTURES

Muslim

Richard Tames

CHILDREN'S PRESS®

A Division of Grolier Publishing

New York London Hong Kong Sydney

Danbury, Connecticut

First American Edition © 1996 by
Children's Press
A Division of Grolier Publishing
Sherman Turnpike
Danbury, Connecticut 06816

Library of Congress Cataloging-in-Publication Data
Tames, Richard.
    Muslim / by Richard Tames.
      p cm — (Beliefs and cultures)
    ISBN: 0-516-08078-4
    1. Islam—Juvenile literature. 2. Muslims—
Juvenile literature. [1. Islam.] I. Title.
    II. Series.
    BP161.2.T35 1995
    297—dc20   94-47347
                    CIP AC

Series Editor: Sarah Ridley
Designer: Liz Black
Copy Editor: Nicola Barber
Picture Researchers: Brooks Krikler
Consultant: Dr. M. Ahsan and the Islamic
Foundation
Photographer (activities): Peter Millard
Illustrators: pages 5 and 20 Aziz Khan; pages 18-
19 Piers Harper.

Photographs: Eye Ubiquitous 24t; Robert Harding Picture
Library 8t, 8b, 10r, 21; Michael Holford cover (left), 6b;
Hutchison Library 13t, 13b, 14t, 24b, 30; ICOREC, Circa
Photo Library, the Manchester Metropolitan University 27b;
Panos Pictures 27t, 28; Richard Tames 6t; Trip cover
(right), 4t, 4b, 7t, 9t, 9b, 10l, 12, 15tl, 15br, 20, 22t,
22b, 23bl, 23tr, 25t, 29.

With thanks also to the IQRA Trust for their help
with this book.

CONTENTS

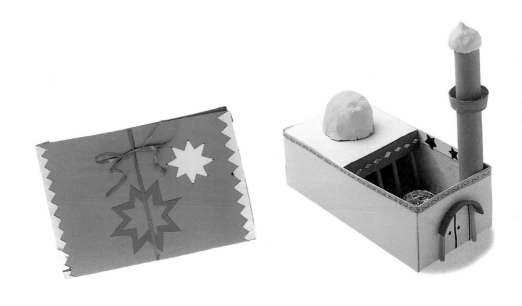

A MAN AND A MESSAGE

Islam is the religion based on the teachings of the Prophet Muhammad, who lived in Arabia about 1,400 years ago. Followers of Islam (an Arabic word meaning "submission" to God) are called Muslims. Islam is the main religion of the Middle East and North Africa, and of countries such as Pakistan, Bangladesh, Indonesia, and Nigeria. However, Muslims have traveled and settled in many countries around the world.

Pilgrims enter the cave on Mount Hira where Muhammad went to think and pray.

The mosque at Medina where Muhammad is buried.

MUHAMMAD

Muhammad was born in the city of Mecca in around 570 CE (CE stands for Common Era). Although he was orphaned as a boy, Muhammad grew up to become a successful merchant. Muhammad could have had an easy life but he was troubled by the evils he saw around him — including greed, cruelty, and superstition. Many of the Arabs were pagans who worshiped idols of wood or stone. Some believed that their tribe was protected by a special god of its own.

Muhammad was a thoughtful man, and he often went into the mountains to think and pray. At the age of forty, he received a revelation (divine message) from God to pass on to the people of Mecca about how they ought to live their lives. These revelations continued to come to Muhammad for the rest of his life and became the words of the *Koran*. God directed him to preach the messages of the Koran to all people.

MUHAMMAD'S TEACHINGS

Muhammad taught that there was only one God and that it was wrong to worship idols. He told people to be kind and generous to the poor and weak, and not to gamble or drink alcohol.

Muhammad's teachings upset many powerful people in Mecca who did not like to be criticized. They also thought that if Muhammad spoke against the worship of idols, then the idol-worshipers might stay away from Mecca and they would lose trade. So Muhammad and his followers were forced to leave the city and settle at the oasis of Medina. For ten years there was war between the people of Mecca and the Muslims. In the end the Muslims were victorious. Muhammad returned to Mecca in triumph and smashed all the idols in the city's main shrine, the *Kaaba*.

After Muhammad's death, in 632 CE, the Muslims spread Islam from Spain to India, and later into Africa and Southeast Asia.

The map shows the percentage of Muslims in the population of each country.

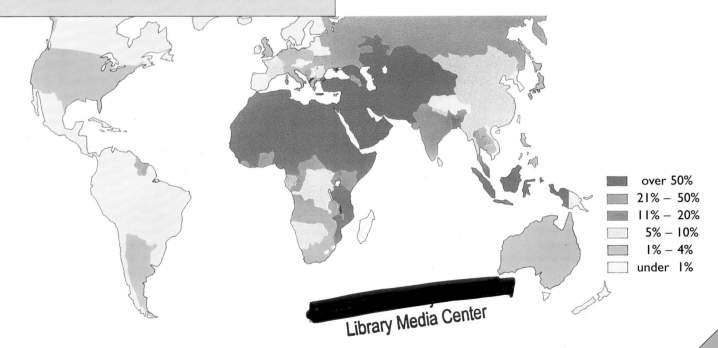

over 50%
21% – 50%
11% – 20%
5% – 10%
1% – 4%
under 1%

THE BELIEFS OF ISLAM

Islam is especially close to two of the other great religions — Judaism and Christianity. All three religions are based on belief in one God and respect for sacred books that record God's teachings. All three command their followers to act with justice and kindness and to show a special care for the poor and weak.

The splendor of sunset proclaims God, the Creator of the world.

Muslims, like Jews, respect Abraham as a prophet and look upon Jerusalem as a holy city. Muslims call Jesus *Isa* and respect him as a true prophet and a great teacher. But, unlike Christians, they do not believe that Jesus is the Son of God or that he died when he was crucified Instead Muslims believe that God took Jesus up off the cross straight into Heaven.

Muslims believe that God sent many prophets to teach people how to lead good lives from the time of Adam, the first man, onward. For Muslims, Muhammad was the "seal of the prophets," the very last one whose words summed up all the important teachings of those who had gone before him.

The Dome on the Rock, Jerusalem, a holy city for Muslims, Jews, and Christians.

THE FIVE PILLARS OF ISLAM

Many Muslims explain Islam as being like a strong building held up by five pillars. The five pillars represent belief, prayer, alms giving, fasting, and pilgrimage.

Muslim men assemble for the Friday noon prayer outside a crowded mosque in Tashkent, Uzbekistan.

☆ BELIEF ☆

The most important belief of Islam can be summed up in one sentence: "*Allah is the only God and Muhammad is His true Messenger.*" *Allah* is the Arabic word for God. This statement of faith is called the *shahada*. It is the first thing whispered into the ear of a Muslim baby at birth. In its written form it is often used as a decoration on walls and works of art.

☆ PRAYER ☆

Muslims should pray five times a day (see pages 12-13).

☆ ALMS ☆

Muslims should give to charity. This money is used to help the poor and support good causes, like education.

☆ FASTING ☆

For one month each year Muslims should go without eating or drinking during daylight (see pages 24-26).

☆ PILGRIMAGE ☆

Once in their lifetimes, Muslims should make a pilgrimage to Mecca, if they can afford it (see pages 20-23).

Almost everyone in this street scene in Istanbul, Turkey, is wearing Western dress.

ISLAM AND THE LAW

Muslim countries vary in how much Islam affects the government and daily life. In Turkey, even though almost everyone is a Muslim, due to Western influence, the law and religion are kept separate and men and women mix together freely in public places.

In Saudi Arabia the Islamic holy book, the Koran (see pages 9-11), is the law. The sexes are kept apart as much as possible, even in schools and colleges. Women cover themselves up almost completely when outside the home, as the Koran commands that they should only uncover themselves before their husbands or young children. In shops and offices, business stops whenever it is time to pray.

In Riyadh, Saudi Arabia, Western dress is the exception. Most men and women do not mix together outside the home.

THE KORAN

When Muhammad preached Islam he spoke in rhyming prose (almost poetry). His teachings were so beautiful that many people believed they could only have come from God. This convinced them that they should become Muslims.

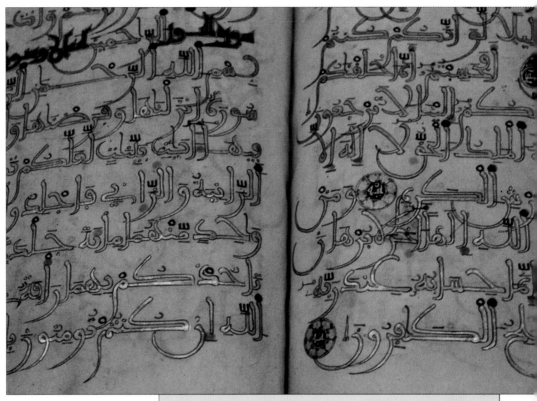

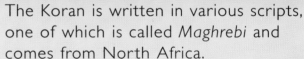

The Koran is written in various scripts, one of which is called *Maghrebi* and comes from North Africa.

This Sudanese boy is learning to write out passages from the Koran.

During Muhammad's lifetime, the words of the Koran, the sacred book of Islam, were collected together. Koran is Arabic for "recitation." The Koran records the words God spoke through the Angel Gabriel to Muhammad to teach people about what they should believe and how they should live. Muslims believe that the Koran records God's actual words. Many copies of the book were made and sent to different parts of the Muslim world.

THE KORAN TODAY

Every Muslim family treats its Koran with great care and respect. It is usually kept wrapped up in a fine cloth and placed on a high shelf, with nothing on top of it. It should be touched only with clean hands. When it is read, it is placed on a rest so that it never touches the ground.

Modern Korans. The making of beautiful books is a living tradition.

Most Muslims read the whole Koran and also learn passages from it as part of their education. Because they believe the Koran to be God's actual words, and therefore perfect, Muslims try to learn at least part of it in the original Arabic. Many Muslims can recite all the 114 chapters by memory. Someone who has learned the whole Koran by heart is known as a *hafiz*.

Some of the most basic rules about Muslim life are laid down in the Koran. These cover what to eat and drink, as well as matters of family life, such as marriage, divorce, and the care of elderly relatives. There is also extra guidance given in the *Hadith*. These are Muhammad's sayings and deeds explaining how to live out the words of the Koran in everyday life.

A Koran class in a Pakistani village, where Arabic is not the native language.

SPOTLIGHT

Some famous Hadith:
- "He is not a true Muslim who eats as much as he wants while his neighbor goes hungry."
- "Someone who helps a widow or a poor person is like a warrior fighting for God."

BEAUTIFUL BOOKS

YOU WILL NEED:

- thin cardboard
- felt-tip pens
- scissors
- colored paper
- ribbon
- glue
- tape
- ruler
- book

WHAT TO DO:

1 Lay your chosen book on the cardboard and draw round it, leaving an extra 1/2 inch to the left and right. Cut along your pencil lines.

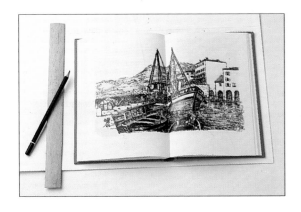

2 Place this cardboard rectangle on colored paper and draw cutting lines roughly 1/2 inch outside the shape. Cut out and glue onto the cardboard.

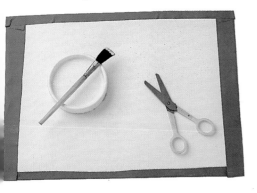

3 Cut out and glue on paper shapes or use felt-tip pens to decorate your book cover.

4 Attach your cover to your book with colored ribbon.

PRAYER

Muslims washing before prayer at the Friday Mosque, Delhi, India, one of the largest mosques in Asia.

DAILY PRAYERS

Muslims are supposed to pray five times a day, facing toward the Kaaba in the holy city of Mecca, wherever they are in the world. The first prayer is said at dawn before sunrise. Other prayers are said at early afternoon, late afternoon, after sunset, and nightfall.

HOW TO PRAY

Before praying, Muslims must wash their hands, arms, feet, and face. This washing is called *wudu*. As they pray, Muslims kneel and bow to show that they are humble before God. The prayers include parts of the Koran and are said in Arabic, even if it is not the person's own language. In these prayers, Muslims praise and thank God and ask for forgiveness and favor. Muslims are also allowed to add personal prayers asking for God's help. These prayers can be said in their own language.

SPOTLIGHT

These words are from the first chapter of the Koran. They are used in every daily prayer.

"Praise be to God.
Lord of the Universe,
the Merciful, the Mercy-giving!
Ruler of the Day
for Repayment!
You do we worship
and from You do we seek help.
Guide us along the
Straight Road, the Road of
those whom You have favored,
with whom You are not angry,
nor who are lost."

WHERE TO PRAY

Prayers can be said anywhere as long as it is clean and, preferably, quiet. On Fridays, Muslims try to go to a mosque for the midday prayer. In many Muslim countries, Friday is a holiday with perhaps a few stores open in the early morning and evening. The prayers of the congregation are led by an *imam*. He is an expert on the Koran and the rules of Islam. Usually on Friday the imam preaches a sermon, explaining what Islam teaches about a current problem or event.

In most Muslim countries women can also go to the mosque, though many prefer to pray at home. In the mosque, women sit separately from men, either at the back or upstairs in a gallery.

Muslims living in a non-Muslim country sometimes have problems keeping strictly to the requirements of their religion. For example, Muslims who work on a factory production line might find it impossible to leave their work to pray, or they may be unable to find a clean, quiet place for prayer. However, many Muslims still try to go to the mosque on Fridays.

Chinese Muslims kneel and bow down in prayer. This shows a believer's submission to Allah (God).

Prayers can be said anywhere that is clean and, preferably, quiet.

MOSQUES

This mosque in Isfahan, Iran, is decorated with stunning tile work. Classes were held in the alcoves.

The Muslim place of worship is a mosque, which means "a place to bow down." In many Muslim towns and villages, mosques are the largest and most beautiful buildings. Some of the most famous mosques are in Cairo in Egypt, Istanbul in Turkey, and Isfahan in Iran.

MINARET AND MUEZZIN

Mosques are often used as schools and places for meetings or celebrations, as well as for worship.

Some mosques have a tall tower, called a minaret. In Muslim countries, this is where the call to prayer comes from. Traditionally, a man known as a *muezzin* stood at the top of the tower to deliver this call, five times a day. Now loud speakers are used as the muezzin calls the people to prayer from inside the mosque, rather than from the minaret. Larger and more important mosques often have a dome. This represents the arch of the heavens

Mosques are all shapes and styles. This mosque in Mali, West Africa, is made of mud brick.

above the Earth, and reminds believers of God's power in making the whole universe.

COURTYARD AND CARPETS
Mosques usually have a large courtyard leading to a covered prayer hall. There is a fountain or faucet where worshipers can wash before praying. Shoes are left outside the prayer hall to keep it clean.

Inside the prayer hall there are no seats, but the floor of the prayer hall is usually covered with carpets. The walls are often decorated with colorful patterns, or with writing

from the Koran. There are no pictures or statues inside the mosque because Muhammad banned them as aids to the worship of idols.

On one wall of the mosque is an alcove called a mihrab. This shows the direction of the Kaaba in Mecca, so that people know the right way to face when they pray. Next to this alcove there is often a kind of pulpit, called a mimbar, from which the imam preaches his sermon, especially on Fridays.

A marble mimbar (pulpit) at the Selimye Mosque, Edirne, Turkey.

MAKING A MOSQUE

YOU WILL NEED:

- shoe box
- cardboard tube
- glue and tape
- modeling clay
- paints and brush
- plastic lid
- orange squeezer
- scissors
- aluminum foil
- drinking straws
- paper cup

WHAT TO DO:

1 Paint the inside and outside of a shoe box to look like brick or pale stone. Leave it to dry.

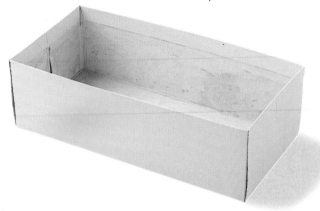

2 Cut the lid into two unequal pieces. Use the shorter piece as the roof of the prayer hall. Paint it to match the rest of the box.

3 Cut the end flap off the remaining part of the lid and glue to the painted roof. Cut drinking straws to make supporting columns and stick inside with tape.

4 Glue the whole roof in place by squeezing it inside the box.

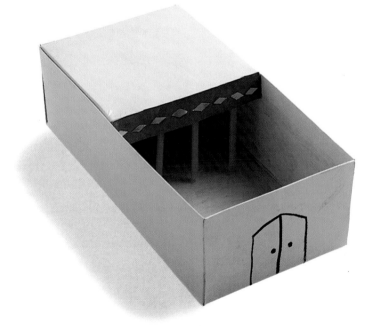

5 To make the dome, cover an orange squeezer with a layer of modeling clay. When it is dry, take it off the orange squeezer and paint it or cover it with aluminum foil. Glue it onto the roof, over the center of the prayer hall.

6 To make the minaret, take the cardboard tube and paint it to match the rest of the mosque. Use the bottom section of a paper cup to make the balcony.

7 Now finish the mosque by making a small dome for the minaret. Use the orange squeezer again but only cover the top part with clay. Again, leave to dry and paint when ready. Glue the whole minaret column in place. Make a washing pool by covering a plastic lid with aluminum foil. Decorate the mosque as you like, with flower or star patterns.

THE FIRST MUEZZIN

There was once a slave, called Bilal, who had a rich and cruel master, named Umayya. When Umayya found out that Bilal had become a Muslim, he tried to force him to go back to worshiping idols.

Umayya tortured Bilal in the desert outside Mecca. He forced him to lie down on the burning sand and placed a huge rock on his chest, so that he could hardly breathe. Then Umayya would say to Bilal, "Give up Islam! Or we'll go on like this until you die!"

As the days passed, Bilal grew weaker but his faith remained strong. However, even though he felt close to death, he still croaked out, "One God, One God..." when Umayya ordered him to give up Islam. Umayya laughed viciously. Bilal was famous for his lovely voice and now he could barely whisper.

One day, a wealthy man named Abu Bakr was walking in the desert and found Bilal in his weak state. Abu Bakr had first taught Bilal about Islam. He turned angrily to Umayya and asked him, "How can you be so cruel? Aren't you afraid of God's anger?"

Umayya replied with a snarl, "I won't be defied by a slave! And, anyway, you're the one to blame for teaching him your religion."

Abu Bakr looked at him calmly now and said, "Very well. If I caused your problem, I will solve it. Sell Bilal to me."

"Glad to and good riddance," snapped Umayya and snatched some gold from Abu Bakr.

Abu Bakr helped Bilal back to Mecca, where he told him that he was no longer a slave. Bilal was now free to follow Islam as he wished. When Muhammad left Mecca for Medina, Bilal went with him.

When they arrived in Medina, the

Muslims built a mosque in which to pray. Medina was not a city like Mecca but an oasis with houses scattered here and there. How could the people be summoned to pray at the mosque? There were plenty of ideas but none of them seemed right to everyone.

Then, one night, one of the Muslims dreamed that he was being called to prayer by a man's voice. On the next day he told Muhammad about his dream.

"I believe God has sent us the answer to our problem," declared the Prophet. But who should do the calling? Many people wanted this honor.

Muhammad knew at once who would be the best — Bilal. Bilal was amazed to be chosen, then delighted, then confused. "I don't know what to say," he said.

"Say only what needs to be said," replied Muhammad.

So Bilal climbed up on to the roof of a house next to the mosque, cupped his hands around his mouth, and boomed out the call to prayer. His rich, deep voice soared over the oasis and the words came out just right:

"*Allahu Akbar* — God is most Great. I declare that there is no god but God. I declare that Muhammad is the messenger of God. Come to prayer. Come to good work."

And so the slave, Bilal, became the first muezzin in the history of Islam.

PILGRIMAGE TO MECCA

Air travel means that people of all ages and many countries can travel to Mecca.

PILGRIM DRESS

When the pilgrims are about six miles outside the city they must wash and change out of their ordinary clothes. Men put on two lengths of unsewn, white cloth. Women usually wear a long robe over their normal clothes. In these unadorned clothes, rich and poor all look alike in the sight of God. Many pilgrims save their pilgrimage garments to be buried in.

Once in their lifetimes all Muslims should go on a pilgrimage to Mecca, as the Koran commands them to if they can. Many then go on to Medina to visit the tombs of Muhammad and other early leaders of Islam. But Muslims should only go on pilgrimage if they are fit and their going does not cause hardship for their families.

The pilgrimage to Mecca is called the *Hajj*. Everyone who completes it can add the word *Hajji* to their name. Over two million pilgrims go to Mecca each year during *Dhu'l Hijja*, the twelfth month in the Muslim calendar, which is the month of pilgrimage.

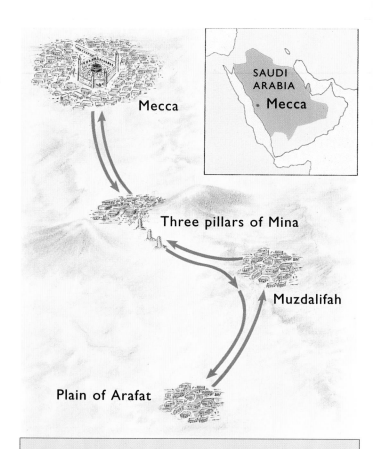

Mecca

SAUDI ARABIA
• Mecca

Three pillars of Mina

Muzdalifah

Plain of Arafat

The pilgrims' route from Mecca.

Pilgrims surround the Kaaba at the heart of Mecca, Saudi Arabia.

CEREMONIES AT SACRED PLACES

When they arrive in Mecca itself, the pilgrims walk seven times counter-clockwise around the sacred house known as the Kaaba. Muslims believe that the Kaaba was built by the prophet Abraham, and that Muhammad's grandfather was its guardian.

Then the pilgrims run seven times between the two low hills of Safa and Marwah. This recalls how Hagar, the ancestor of the Arab people, ran about the desert, looking for water for her son, Ishmael.

The pilgrims go to the Plain of Arafat. There, the pilgrims stand for

For one day in the year, the Plain of Arafat is a tented city of two million people.

a whole afternoon in the hot sun, praying and begging forgiveness for their sins. Muslims believe that it was here Adam and Eve had their sins forgiven by God.

STONING AND SACRIFICE

After spending the afternoon at Arafat, the pilgrims go to Muzdalifah to camp overnight and to gather pebbles. The next day, the pilgrims go to the village of Mina where they throw the pebbles at three stone pillars as a symbol of Abraham's rejection of the Devil. At Mina an

Pilgrims collecting stones at Muzdalifah, to throw at the pillars.

INTERVIEW
Some of my friends from college thought we were mad, spending our money on a pilgrimage before we had paid for our house and car. But Allah doesn't tell us we have to have a house and a car. He tells us to go to Mecca if we can afford it.

Soleiman Abdullah, aged 32, Kuala Lumpur, Malaysia.

animal is sacrificed as an offering to God, and the meat is given away to the poor. Most pilgrims pay a professional butcher to do this. Then men have their heads shaved and women cut off at least 1/2 inch of their hair.

At the end of their pilgrimage, the pilgrims go around the Kaaba another seven times. Many then go

Pilgrims touch the Kaaba one last time before their journey home.

on to the city of Medina to visit the mosque of the prophet Muhammad. The pilgrims return home with many souvenirs of their visit, such as zam-zam (holy water), prayer beads, or prayer carpets to give to their families and friends.

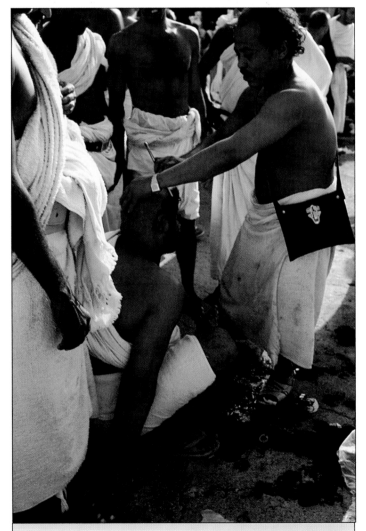

Shaving the head is a symbol of giving up personal vanity on the pilgrimage.

SPOTLIGHT

The Kaaba is a cube-like building that now stands at the heart of Mecca's main mosque. Muslims believe that it was originally built by Adam, then later rebuilt by Abraham and his son Ishmael. As they were working on it, they were given a black stone by the Angel Gabriel that they built into one corner. Pilgrims try to touch or kiss the black stone as they walk round the Kaaba.

FEASTING AND FASTING

Meal times are important as a way of gathering the whole family together, particularly at the end of Ramadan.

THE FAST OF RAMADAN

The ninth month of the Muslim calendar is called *Ramadan*. This is when Muhammad first began to hear revelations (messages) from God. Muslims remember this important event by fasting through the hours of daylight. This means not eating or drinking anything — to fast properly a person should not even take a sip of water. This is very hard to do in hot countries, where many Muslims live. In non-Muslim countries, keeping to a fast can be even harder. For example, Muslim children at school in non-Muslim countries might find it difficult to fast when friends all around them are eating snacks and lunches.

Muslims break their fast after sunset, when the whole family gathers to eat. Another meal is eaten just before dawn. Pregnant women, young children, and very old people do not fast, nor do people who are ill, traveling, or in combat.

FEASTING AT FESTIVALS

Two great festivals — *Eid al-Fitr* and *Eid al-Adha* — are celebrated by feasting, visiting relatives, and giving presents. Eid al-Fitr means "Festival of Fast-breaking," and it comes at the end of the month of Ramadan. Eid al-Adha means "Festival of Sacrifice." It is celebrated at the time when Muslims go on pilgrimage to Mecca (see pages 20-23).

Prayers to mark the end of Ramadan in Cameroon, West Africa.

24

London children being given sweets to celebrate Eid al-Fitr.

HALAL AND HARAM

Muslims live in many different countries around the world, so they eat many different kinds of food. But all Muslims are forbidden by the Koran to eat certain things. Foods that are forbidden by the Koran are called *haram* (banned). Foods that are permitted and have been properly prepared are *halal* (lawful).

Haram items include anything made from a pig; meat with blood still in it; meat or fat from an animal that has not been killed correctly; and meat from a flesh-eating animal or an animal sacrificed to idols. Pig products include not only pork, ham, and bacon but many other foodstuffs that contain pork fat, such as biscuits, ice cream, and soups.

Muslims are also forbidden to drink alcoholic drinks such as beer, wine, or whiskey.

For an animal's meat to be halal, it must be killed by having the main vein in its neck cut with a sharp knife while the butcher pronounces the name of God. This is to show that the life of one of God's creatures is not being taken thoughtlessly.

In a real emergency, if no other food can be found, Muslims are allowed to eat even foods which are haram rather than starve to death.

INTERVIEW

I began trying to fast when I was about seven. Because we all have a big meal just before it gets light, it isn't so bad going without food. The hardest part is not drinking at all. When I came here from Morocco I thought it would be easier because it wasn't so hot. But here most people aren't Muslims, so there are cooking smells and people eating all around you.
Muhammad El-Baja, aged 13
London, UK.

MAKING A FRUIT DRINK

Many Muslims live in hot countries where iced fruit or yogurt drinks are very refreshing, particularly during the month of fasting.

YOU WILL NEED
- 5 oranges
- ice cubes
- sharp knife
- 1 tablespoon sugar (optional)
- glasses
- sieve
- orange squeezer
- jug
- saucepan

WHAT TO DO:

1 Carefully cut the oranges in half. Using an orange squeezer, squeeze the juice out of them and into a jug.

2 Using the sieve, remove the seeds and pulp from the juice.

3 (Skip this stage if you don't want to add sugar.) Add the sugar and heat the orange juice and sugar in a saucepan until the sugar has dissolved.

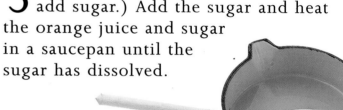

4 Serve with lots of ice and enjoy the drink.

THE MUSLIM FAMILY

A family enjoying themselves on a beach in Kuwait. The Muslim woman's main role is to bring up a happy family.

The family lies at the heart of Islam. The Koran gives special attention to the care of widows and orphans, whose families have been broken up by death.

The health and happiness of a family depends mainly on the mother. Her work in the home is considered to be just as important as the father's job. His main tasks are to provide the family with income and protection. Both parents have a duty to teach their children about Islam. Children should be learning to pray and fast by the time they are seven years old. Muslim children are expected to show respect to their parents and to look after them when they get old.

CUSTOMS AND CEREMONIES

The customs affecting birth, marriage, and death vary in different parts of the Muslim world. But basic rules are widely accepted.

BIRTH

A child is regarded as a gift from God, and Muslims think a large family is a great blessing. The first words a baby hears are about God: "*Allah is the only God and Muhammad is his true Messenger.*" About seven days after birth, the baby is named and its head is shaved. The name often comes from a person famous in the history of Islam. All Muslim boys are circumcised. A Muslim doctor performs a simple operation to cut

Babies are named at a special ceremony, where their heads are also shaved.

the foreskin off the boy's penis. This may be done a few days after birth, or years later.

MARRIAGE

Marriage is seen as the joining together of two families, not just two people. Therefore parents often guide their children as to whom they will marry. However, they do not force their children to accept their choice. Muslims believe that love often becomes stronger when it grows out of an arranged marriage, rather than coming before it.

The simple wedding ceremony is made up of readings from the Koran and prayers. It is often led by

Different styles of dress at a Muslim wedding in Turkey.

an imam, but does not have to be as long as there are two adult male witnesses. The bride, groom, and guests often wear splendid clothes and jewelry, give gifts, and celebrate with a delicious meal. In some countries, a procession carries the bride from her parents' home to the home of her new husband. Divorce is permitted but is "the most hateful of all permitted things."

DEATH AND BURIAL

Muslims believe that after death they will be judged by God on the Day of Judgment when history comes to an end. Each person will be sent to heaven or hell according to how they lived their lives.

When someone dies, the family washes the body for burial. Burial should follow as quickly as possible after death. Cremation (burning the body) is forbidden since the dead will have their bodies restored to life at the Day of Judgment, and cremation is seen as a desecration of the body. Funerals should be simple and dignified. The body is buried with the face turned toward Mecca. Rather than spend money on expensive gravestones, Muslims give the money to the poor.

The tombs of the faithful are aligned with Mecca at this cemetery in Tunisia.

STARS IN THE SKY

When Prophet Muhammad met people who refused to believe in God, he would point to the sky and ask them who they thought had made the stars and planets. The regular movements of these heavenly bodies in the sky have often been taken as proof that the whole Universe follows an order set down by God. Patterns based on the constellations are often used to decorate mosques and Islamic works of art.

ASTRONOMY

Throughout history, Muslim scholars have taken a great interest in astronomy, the study of the stars, and planets. Many stars have Arabic names such as Aldebaran ("the following"), or Algol ("the destruction"). In the past, astronomy had many practical uses. It allowed sailors to find their way across the oceans when they were out of sight of land. Travelers in the great deserts, where there were no reliable landmarks, could also steer by the stars to avoid getting hopelessly lost. The study of the stars and planets was also essential for making an accurate calendar and fixing the correct direction of prayer.

THE MUSLIM CALENDAR

The Muslim calendar is based on the movements of the Moon rather than the Sun. This means that the Muslim year is eleven days shorter than the year according to the calendar used in Western countries. The Western calendar begins with the birth of Jesus and is moving toward the 21st century. The Muslim calendar began when Muhammad moved from Mecca to Medina. It is now in its 15th century.

An 18th-century observatory in India. Many stars have Arabic names.

DECORATED PLATES

WHAT TO DO:

1 Take your pencil and mark out two sets of lines, as shown here.

2 Join the lines together in whichever way you want to produce a star. Experiment to produce different types of stars. Mark out how many different areas you want to color in.

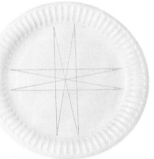

3 Color in your pattern to make a decorative plate. Patterns like this are used in Islamic art on mosques and other buildings. Sometimes these star patterns are very complicated.

31

GLOSSARY

Allah Arabic for God.
Congregation group of worshipers gathered for prayer.
Constellations groups of stars.
Cremation burning a dead body to reduce it to ashes.
Fasting going without food or drink as an act of religious discipline.
Hadith a record of traditional sayings about what the Prophet Muhammad said, or did, or approved of.
Hafiz a person who has memorized all of the Koran.
Hajj pilgrimage to Mecca.
Halal something permitted by Islamic law.
Haram something forbidden by Islamic law.
Idol a man-made figure, usually of stone, wood, or metal, worshiped in the mistaken belief that it is holy.
Imam leader of Muslim congregation at prayer.
Islam the religion of Muslims; Islam means submitting to the will of God.
Judaism the Jewish religion.
Mihrab niche in a mosque wall showing the direction of prayer toward Mecca.

Minaret tower attached to a mosque, from which Muslims are often called to prayer by a muezzin.
Mimbar pulpit with stairs from which a sermon is preached at the Friday midday prayer.
Mosque building for the worship of Allah, also often used for meetings and teaching.
Muezzin official who calls Muslims to prayer.
Muslim a follower of Islam.
Oasis a well-watered, fertile patch of land in a desert region.
Orphaned losing one's parents.
Pagan a believer in idols or false gods.
Pilgrimage journey to a holy place.
Prophet a teacher with a message from God.
Recitation saying something out loud.
Revelation a message from God.
Shrine holy place for worship, often associated with a particular person.
Superstition a false belief.
Tomb burial place.
Wudu act of washing before prayer.

INDEX